US Army Technical Center for Explosives Safety

TACTICAL EXPLOSIVES SAFETY

Quick Reference Guide

Revision 6
15 December 2011

US Army Technical Center for Explosives Safety
DSN 956-8737 or commercial (918) 420-8737
usarmy.mcalester.usamc.list.dac-es

The Cardinal Rule

Expose:

the **minimum number of people**

to the **minimum amount of explosives**

for the **minimum amount of time**

Consistent with **safe and efficient** operations.

TACTICAL EXPLOSIVES SAFETY
Quick Reference Guide

Revision 6
15 December 2011

Table of Contents

Purpose 6

Introduction 7

Distances 8

    Quantity Distance 8

    Measuring Distances 9

    Internal Distances 9

    External Distances 12

Barricades 16

    Barricade Diagram 17

Blast/Fragment Effects Chart Unbarricaded 18

Blast/Fragment Effects Chart Barricaded 19

Hazard Classification 20

Net Explosive Weight (NEW) 25

Storage Compatibility 27

    Storage Compatibility Mixing Chart 28

Ammo Storage Areas 29

    Storage Sites 29

BLAHA Storage Table of Distances.......................................33

BLAHA Storage Distances Diagram 34

AHA Configuration 36

Earth-Filled Steel Bin Barricades.....................................37

Steel Bin Barricade Diagram...39

Arms Rooms...40

Light Armor Vehicles...41

Light Armor Vehicles Table of Distances 43

Forward Arming and Refueling Point (FARP)....................44

FARP Diagram 45

Combat Aircraft Parking Area (CAPA)................................46

Certificate of Risk Acceptance (CoRA) 48

Explosives Licenses 51

Explosives Safety Assistance 53

Acronyms 54

Glossary 57

Purpose

Purpose

The purpose of this guide is to provide personnel, in possession of ammunition and explosives (A&E), information on how to manage the risks associated with A&E storage and handling; it is designed for use by personnel who have had academic exposure to the concepts herein.

The general information contained in this guide regards typical ammunition storage and handling activities, and meets criteria contained in Army Regulation (AR) 385-10, The Army Safety Program, DA PAM 385-64, Ammunition and Explosives Safety Standards and DA PAM 385-30, Mishap Risk Management.

A&E will be referred to as ammo in the contents of this guide.

Introduction

Separation distances provide protection against effects of blast or overpressure, high speed, low angle fragmentation and fire from accidental or enemy action. The greater the distance from a potential explosion site (PES), the greater protection the exposed site (ES) is afforded. Protection from fragments can also be provided by properly constructed and located barricades.

When possible, all ammo should be stored in its original packaging in a designated ammo storage area. Original packaging may provide greater protection from the effects of detonation and may prevent the ammo from contributing to the detonation.

It is imperative that the proper degree of protection is provided for personnel and assets. A lesser distance, and thus lesser protection, is acceptable risk for related personnel and operations directly associated with the ammo storage area mission. A greater distance and a higher level of protection is required for all other personnel. Examples of <u>unrelated</u> personnel or operations requiring a <u>higher</u> degree of protection are:

- Dining facilities
- AAFES
- Barracks
- Medical facilities
- MWR facilities

Distances

Quantity Distance

The application of the rules on separation is called Quantity Distance (QD).

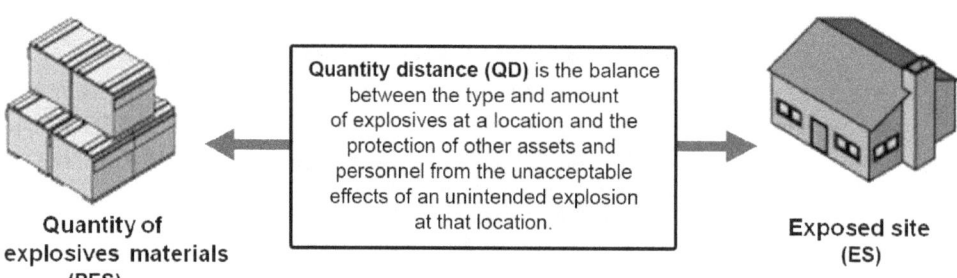

Quantity distance (QD) is the balance between the type and amount of explosives at a location and the protection of other assets and personnel from the unacceptable effects of an unintended explosion at that location.

Quantity of explosives materials (PES)

Exposed site (ES)

QD relationships are based on levels of risk considered acceptable for specific exposures. These relationships are tabulated in applicable QD tables.

- These separation distances do **not** provide absolute safety or protection.
- **Greater** distances than those in the QD tables should be used if possible.

Measuring Distances

Distances should be measured from the exterior edge of any ammo or ammo container to the nearest edge of any site exposed to the ammo.

Internal Distances

Internal distances are those required for the separation of operating facilities and storage sites within the confines of an ammo storage area. Internal distances are the minimum required by DA PAM 385-64 and Technical Data Packages approved by the Department of Defense Explosives Safety Board (DDESB).

Intermagazine Distance

Intermagazine Distance (IMD) is the distance required between two ammo storage locations, such as pads within an Ammunition Supply Point (ASP) or Ammunition Holding Area (AHA).

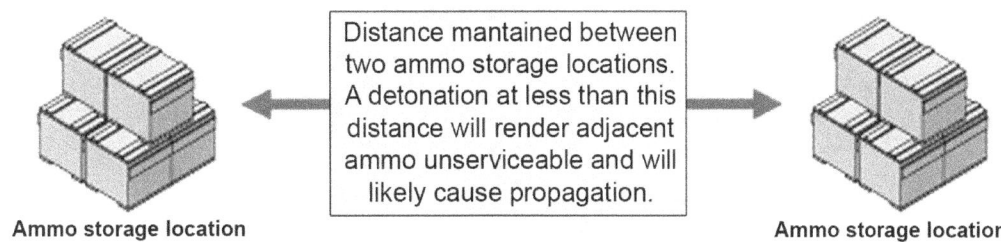

Ammo storage location

Distance mantained between two ammo storage locations. A detonation at less than this distance will render adjacent ammo unserviceable and will likely cause propagation.

Ammo storage location

Intraline Distance

Intraline Distance (ILD) is the distance to be maintained from a PES, such as a pad within an ASP, to an associated ES, such as ammo surveillance or ammo maintenance. ILD can be barricaded (B) or unbarricaded (U).

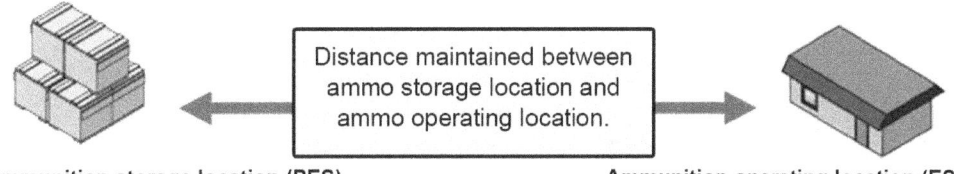

Ammunition storage location (PES)

Distance maintained between ammo storage location and ammo operating location.

Ammunition operating location (ES)

IMD and ILD are adjusted based on the presence or absence of properly designed and constructed barricades (see Barricades section). These internal distances are expected to prevent ammo stack A from instantly detonating ammo stack B. Delayed propagation of an explosives event to adjacent storage locations is still possible.

Expected Effects

It is extremely important that applicable internal distances are established and maintained between explosives locations.

If these distances are not maintained, an explosive event can be expected to propagate rapidly between sites, resulting in the destruction of all ammunition and explosives assets and rendering the unit incapable of performing its mission and denying access to the area until EOD can render safe damaged items.

Although prompt propagation is not expected, collateral damage to ammunition on nearby storage sites and operating facilities may be so severe that the assets may become unserviceable.

Providing a greater distance than the minimum standard will provide greater protection and survivability to the nearby assets.

Before

After

External Distances

External distances are those required for the separation of personnel and facilities that are outside the confines of an ammo storage area and that are not directly related or associated with the ammo storage area mission.

These external distances are identified as:
- Inhabited Building Distance (IBD)
- Public Traffic Route Distance (PTRD)

Examples of IBD are installation boundary, dining facilities, billeting, MWR facilities, medical facilities, tactical operations center, fuel/water storage, and other life support facilities.

Examples of PTRD are on-base roads (external to ammo area), power lines, navigable rivers, open-air recreational facilities and open-air training ranges. **Generally PTRD is 60% IBD.**

Realistically, the required distances described are not always possible to obtain in a deployment situation. In the initial deployment, Commanders must follow FM 5-19 and use composite risk management to identify and minimize the risk to personnel and mission capability. Once the situation has stabilized, efforts should be made to comply with QD requirements; consideration should be given to moving personnel and material assets that are at risk from the ammunition being stored or establishing a new ammunition facility. If QD compliance is still not possible, a DA Form 7632, Certificate of Risk Acceptance (CoRA) must be initiated. CoRAs are explained later in this guide.

Inhabited Building Distance

IBD provides excellent protection to personnel and material assets from blast effects and very good protection from fragments at this level of protection. There is moderate risk of serious injury and possible fatalities from rogue fragments.

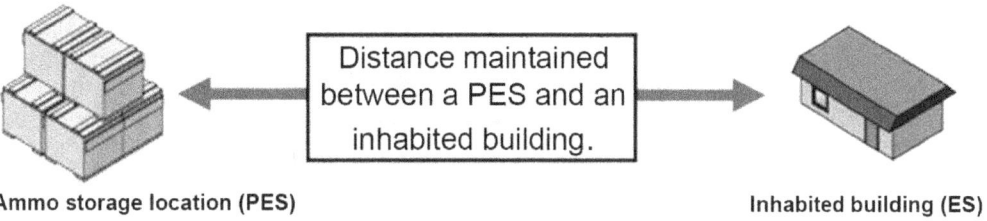

Ammo storage location (PES)   Inhabited building (ES)

Public Traffic Route Distance

PTRD provides less protection with a higher probability of serious injuries and fatalities than does inhabited building distance. Most material assets at PTRD can be expected to be serviceable or easily repairable.

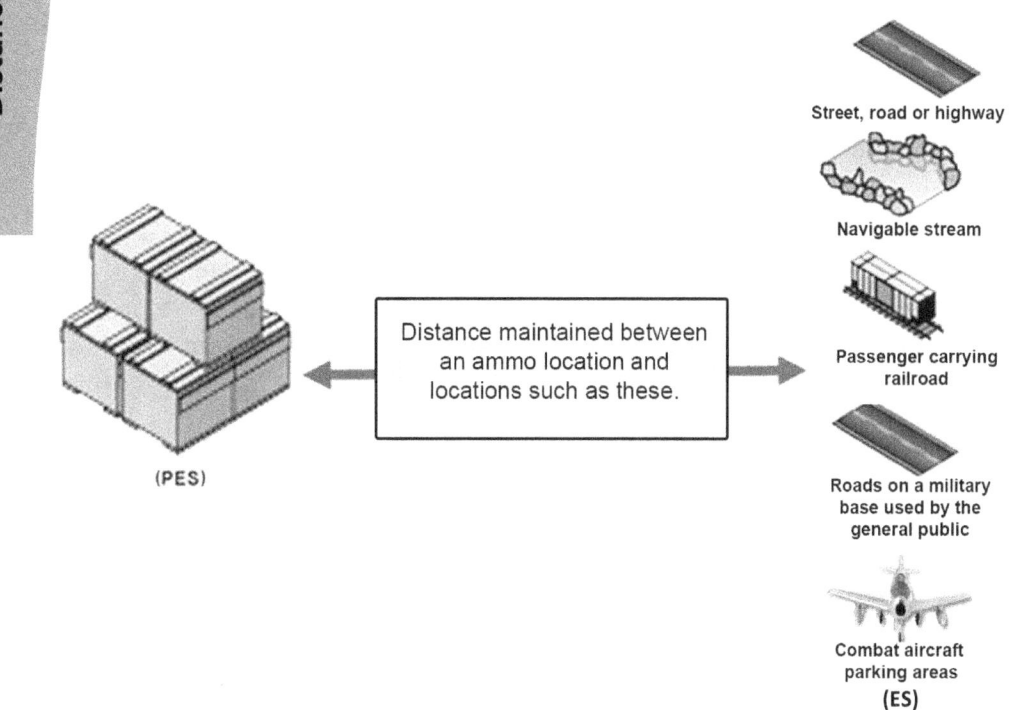

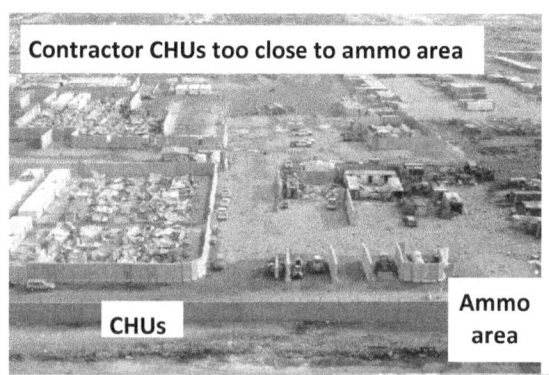

Contractor CHUs too close to ammo area

CHUs

Ammo area

FOB Falcon Iraq, 2006, incoming round, excess ammo present, ammo stored for weapon system not present. Contractor CHUs too near ammo location flattened.

Ammo area destroyed

Barricades

Properly constructed and located barricades reduce the internal footprint (IM/IL distances) of an AHA or any other ammo operation or site. They do not reduce the external footprint. Barricades will stop high velocity, low angle fragments but are ineffective in preventing high, lobbed fragments. For this reason, there is no reduction in the external distance (IBD/PTRD) based on the presence of barricades.

Barricades are typically built of earth construction. Typically, barricades do not use concrete, heavy steel, stones or debris heavier than 10 lb or larger than 6 inches in diameter in the fill or cover due to the added fragmentation or spalling hazard they create. A natural land feature can be used as a barricade provided there is line-of-sight PLUS 1 foot between the ammo locations, and the top of the natural feature is at least 1 foot thick. HESCO Concertainer barricades have been used to provide the requirements of a properly constructed barricade.

The barricade diagram shows general details of a barricade. Properly designed barricades use a 2:1 ratio (2 feet of run for every 1 foot of rise). A MIL 7 topped by a MIL 4 HESCO works well for this configuration.

DO NOT USE STONES IN BARRICADE FILL.

Barricade Diagram

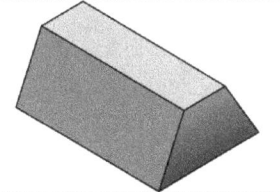

0.3m Min.

STACK   Barricade   STACK

0.3m Min.

STACK   MIL 4 & MIL 7 HESCOS   STACK

CONCRETE BARRIERS (i.e. T-Walls, Texas or Jersey Barriers, etc.)
DO NOT provide "BARRICADE" protection for explosives safety purposes. They may be of value for Force Protection, but do not reduce QD
requirements.

Blast/Fragment Effects Chart Unbarricaded

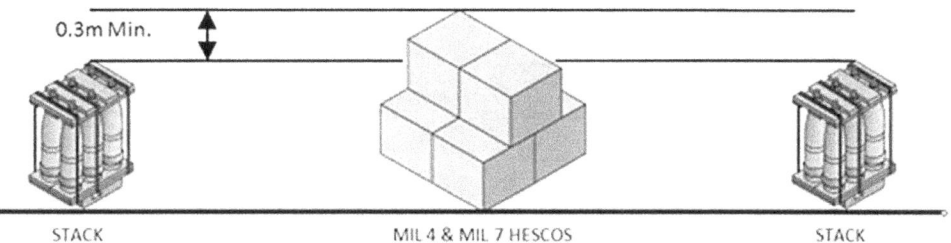

| | Distance in Feet | 0 | 228 | 372 | 750 | 1,250 | Maximum Hazardous Fragment Distance |
| | | | 228 | 372 | 496 | 827 | Blast Only Distance |

EFFECTS	EFFECTS	EFFECTS	EFFECTS	EFFECTS
• Personnel Killed by blast • Aircraft Destroyed by blast and fragments • Vehicles Overturned and crushed • Buildings Destroyed by blast	• Personnel Seriously injured or killed by blast and fragments • Aircraft Heavily damaged • Vehicles Severely damaged • Buildings Damaged to near destruction	• Personnel Seriously injured by frag; 2% chance eardrum damage • Aircraft Structural damage • Vehicles Extensively damaged • Buildings Damaged - 50% of replacement cost	• Personnel Minor to moderate injury by fragments and building debris • Aircraft Minor structural damage, fragment penetration possible • Vehicles Minor damage • Buildings Damaged - 20% of replacement cost	• Personnel Minor injury from building debris and flying glass • Aircraft Minor fragment damage possible • Vehicle Minor fragment damage possible • Buildings Damaged - 5% of replacement cost
TOTAL DESTRUCTION				NO SIGNIFICANT EFFECTS

KILLED   SERIOUS INJURIES   INJURIES LIKELY   INJURIES POSSIBLE

DESTROYED   MAJOR AIRFRAME DAMAGE   MINOR AIRFRAME DAMAGE   OPERATIONAL

AMMO STRG

DAMAGED
NO IMMEDIATE
PROPAGATION *

EXTENSIVE BODY DAMAGE   MINOR DAMAGE   OPERATIONAL

8,818 POUNDS

DESTROYED

DESTROYED   SERIOUS DAMAGE   MODERATE DAMAGE   OPERATIONAL

Type Distance ⟶ IMD(U)   ILD(U)   PTRD   IBD

ASSET LOSS   ASSET PROTECTION

DESTROYED   NOT MISSION CAPABLE   COMBAT EFFECTIVE

* Delayed Propagation is possible from fire and firebrands (lobbed or projected flaming debris). Prompt Propagation (sympathetic detonation) of PACKAGED AMMO is not likely.
NOTE – The effects shown in each column are the effects that can be expected at or near the distance on the left side of the column and will diminish with increased distance.

Blast/Fragment Effects Chart Barricaded

THESE DISTANCES ARE NOT DECREASED BY BARRICADING

0	124			

Distance in Feet   124

EFFECTS	EFFECTS	EFFECTS	EFFECTS	EFFECTS
Personnel Killed by blast **Aircraft** Destroyed by blast and fragments **Vehicles** Overturned and crushed **Buildings** Destroyed by blast	**Personnel** Seriously injured or killed by blast and fragments **Aircraft** Heavily damaged **Vehicles** Severely damaged **Buildings** Damaged to near destruction	**Personnel** Seriously injured by frag, 2% chance eardrum damage **Aircraft** Structural damage **Vehicles** Extensively damaged **Buildings** Damaged - 50% of replacement cost	**Personnel** Minor to moderate injury by fragments and building debris **Aircraft** Minor structural damage, fragment penetration possible **Vehicles** Minor damage **Buildings** Damaged - 20% of replacement cost	**Personnel** Minor injury from building debris and flying glass **Aircraft** Minor fragment damage possible **Vehicle** Minor fragment damage possible **Buildings** Damaged - 5% of replacement cost
TOTAL DESTRUCTION				NO SIGNIFICANT EFFECTS

	KILLED	SERIOUS INJURIES	INJURIES LIKELY	INJURIES POSSIBLE
8,818 POUNDS **Barricade**	DESTROYED	MAJOR AIRFRAME DAMAGE	MINOR AIRFRAME DAMAGE	OPERATIONAL
	AMMO STRG — DAMAGED NO IMMEDIATE PROPAGATION *	EXTENSIVE BODY DAMAGE	MINOR DAMAGE	OPERATIONAL
	DESTROYED			
	DESTROYED	SERIOUS DAMAGE	MODERATE DAMAGE	OPERATIONAL

Type Distance ➡	IMD(B)	ILD(U)**	PTRD	IBD

	ASSET LOSS	ASSET PROTECTION
DESTROYED	**NOT MISSION CAPABLE**	**COMBAT EFFECTIVE**

* Delayed Propagation is possible from fire and firebrands (lobbed or projected flaming debris). Prompt Propagation (sympathetic detonation) of PACKAGED AMMO is not likely.

** ILD(B) is not shown due to limited application.

Hazard Classification

The <u>official</u> source for determining the Hazard Class/Division (HCD) and the Net Explosive Weight (NEW) for ammo items is the Joint Hazard Classification System (JHCS) available at (requires login and password): https://www3.dac.army.mil/esidb/login/

An <u>unofficial</u> source for HCD and NEW is the "Yellow Book" available by email request to: mcal.dac.yellowbook@conus.army.mil

HAZARD CLASSIFICATION
OF
UNITED STATES MILITARY
EXPLOSIVES AND MUNITIONS

U.S. ARMY
DEFENSE AMMUNITION CENTER

LOGISTICS REVIEW
and
TECHNICAL ASSISTANCE
OFFICE

REVISION 14
1 JUNE 2009

Using the "Yellow Book"

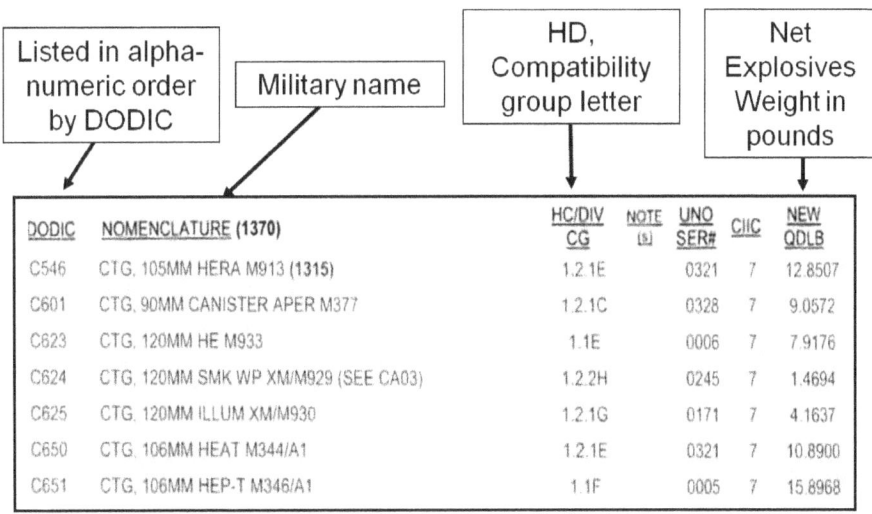

Listed in alpha-numeric order by DODIC

Military name

HD, Compatibility group letter

Net Explosives Weight in pounds

DODIC	NOMENCLATURE (1370)	HC/DIV CG	NOTE [s]	UNO SER#	CIIC	NEW QDLB
C546	CTG, 105MM HERA M913 (1315)	1.2.1E		0321	7	12.8507
C601	CTG, 90MM CANISTER APER M377	1.2.1C		0328	7	9.0572
C623	CTG, 120MM HE M933	1.1E		0006	7	7.9176
C624	CTG, 120MM SMK WP XM/M929 (SEE CA03)	1.2.2H		0245	7	1.4694
C625	CTG, 120MM ILLUM XM/M930	1.2.1G		0171	7	4.1637
C650	CTG, 106MM HEAT M344/A1	1.2.1E		0321	7	10.8900
C651	CTG, 106MM HEP-T M346/A1	1.1F		0005	7	15.8968

This is a typical data page from the Yellow Book. A DODIC is a 4 digit alphanumeric designation for the different types of ammo. Nomenclature is the "military" name for it. The column headed "HC/DIV CG" contains information used to determine the hazard associated with an ammo item and types of ammo that can be located together. The "NEW QDLB" column has Information that is used to determine how much ammo may be placed i
n any given location. How these types of information are used is discussed in other portions of the booklet.

The DOD uses the international system of classification devised by the United Nations Organization (UNO) for transport of dangerous goods. The UNO classification system consists of nine Hazard Classes (HC). Class 1 contains most ammunition and explosive items. The hazard division is a numerical designator within an HC indicating an item's associated hazards and potential for causing casualties and property damage. For example, within HC 1 (explosives), there are six divisions. The first four are listed below.

Division 1.1—Explosives that have a mass explosion hazard, i.e., a mass explosion effects the entire load instantaneously.

Examples include artillery projectiles, frag grenades and some types of missiles.

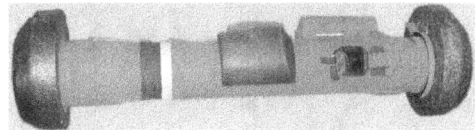

Division 1.2—High explosives filled items that, when one detonates, it is expected that NOT all the others in the same location will explode at the same time. This presents fragment hazard.

Examples include some types of mortar rounds, linked ammo and simulators.

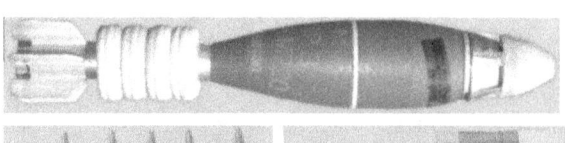

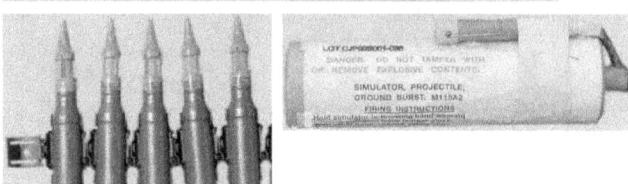

Division 1.3—Ammo that has a significant fire hazard. When started, the fire typically cannot be put out. This may have a minor fragment or explosion hazard.

Examples include propelling charges, signals and rocket motors.

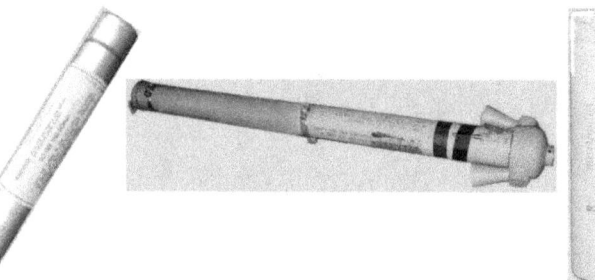

Division 1.4—Ammo that has a relatively minor explosion hazard.

Some types include signal cartridges, and ammo for pistols, rifles, shotguns, and machine guns.

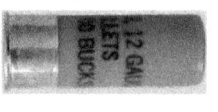

Net Explosive Weight

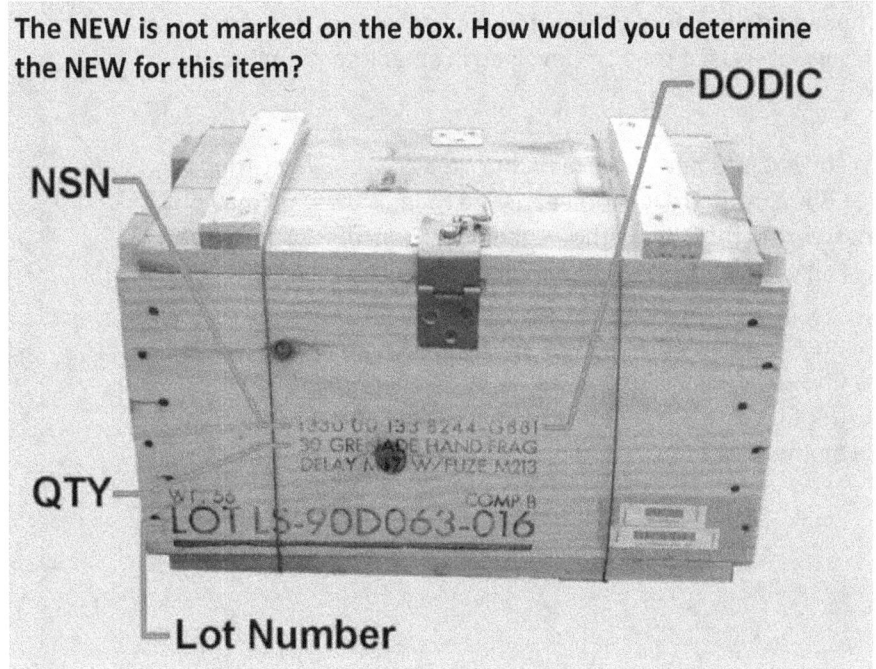

The NEW is not marked on the box. How would you determine the NEW for this item?

DODIC

NSN

NEW

QTY

LOT LS-90D063-016

Lot Number

Determining NEW

Based on the DODIC G881:

NEW

1. Identify the amount of ammo: **2 boxes @ 30 rounds per box**

   2 X 30 = **60 rounds**

2. Locate the NEW in the JHCS or Yellow Book:

DODIC	Nomenclature (1310)	HC/DIV CG	Note (s)	UNO SER#	CIIC	NEW QDLB	NEW QDKG
G878	FUZE, HAND GREN M228 (1330)	1.4B		0257	4	0.0045	0.0020
G880	GRENADE. HAND FRAG M61	(04)1.1F		0292	2	0.3787	0.1718
G881	**GRENADE, HAND FRAG M67**	(04)1.1F		0292	2	0.4137	0.1876
G890	GRENADE. HAND FRAG MK2/M26 SER	(*)1.1F		0292	2	0.3900	0.1769
	00-301-1970, * (N/A); ALL OTHERS, * (04)						
G892	GRENADE. HAND FRAG MK2A1	1.1F		0292	2	0.1000	0.0454

Excerpted from the Yellow Book, page 58

3. Multiply: **60 X 0.4137 lb = 24.83 lb**

Storage Compatibility

Ammo is grouped into hazard divisions to accurately indicate their damage causing potential if they are involved in an unintentional detonation or fire.

It is also categorized into one of thirteen Storage Compatibility Groups (SCG). The SCG is a letter designation assigned to indicate what may be stored or transported together without significantly increasing either the probability of an accident or the magnitude of an accident's effects.

The SCG assigned to a particular type of ammo can also be found in the Joint Hazard Classification System or Yellow Book under the column headed "HC/DIV CG". It is the letter following hazard classification. Using the example on the previous page, the SCG for G881 is "F".

Storage Compatibility Mixing Chart

Storage Compatibility

GROUP	A	B	C	D	E	F	G	H	J	K	L	N	S
A	X	Z											
B	Z	X	Z	Z	Z	Z	Z					X	X
C		Z	X	X	X	Z	Z					X	X
D		Z	X	X	X	Z	Z					X	X
E		Z	X	X	X	Z	Z					X	X
F		Z	Z	Z	Z	X	Z					Z	X
G		Z	Z	Z	Z	Z	X					Z	X
H								X					X
J									X				X
K										Z			
L											*		
N		X	X	X	X	Z	Z					X	X
S		X	X	X	X	X	X	X	X			X	X

Excerpt from the Yellow Book, page E1

TABLE NOTES - from DA PAM 385-64

A Draft-Revision to DA PAM 385-64 contains changes to the below notes and appears in Chapter 7.
1. "X" at the intersection of a row and column indicates that items assigned to those SCG may be stored together; otherwise, mixing is either prohibited or restricted according to note #2.
2. "Z" at the intersection of a row and column indicates that, those two SCG may not be stored together without the proper permission. When such conditions as operational considerations or magazine nonavailability and when safety is not sacrificed, logical mixed storage of limited quantities of some items of different groups may be approved. These relaxations involving mixed storage shall be approved by the MACOM and are not considered waivers.
3. Mixed storage of 4,000 kg or less combined net explosives weight of various types of ammo is authorized without regard to compatibility, except that items in SGC "L" cannot be stored with other items.

Ammo Storage Areas

Storage Sites

Storage areas can include:

MILVANS   **ISO Containers**   **Open Pads**   **ARMAG Containers**

Operating facilities (in the open or in structures) can include:

- Workshops
- Reconfiguration (pack/unpack/repack) operations
- Minor maintenance operations
- Issue/turn-in operations
- Administrative office spaces directly related to the ammo mission

There are two general types of ammo *storage areas* in a contingency environment:

- Ammunition Holding Areas (AHA) - Areas where ammo has already been issued to the unit or troops
  - ◆ Basic Load Ammunition Holding Areas (BLAHA)
  - ◆ Ammunition Transfer and Holding Areas (ATHP)
  - ◆ Aviation AHAs (Avn AHA)
  - ◆ Artillery AHAs (Arty AHA)

- Ammunition Supply Points (ASP) - Areas where ammo has not been issued to the unit or troops
  - ◆ Theater Storage Areas (TSA)
  - ◆ Corps Storage Areas (CSA)

AHA Storage

AHA storage sites (also known as BLAHA, ATHP, Avn AHA, Arty AHA, etc.) are locations where ammo that has been issued to units can be safely stored. They may consist of one or more storage sites and involve acceptance of risks to personnel, facilities and equipment that are greater than normally permitted. An AHA storage site can be an open pad, uploaded vehicle, MILVAN or ISO container, barricaded cell, etc.

The concept of BLAHA storage may also be used to provide QD separations during mobile operations. The maximum NEW at any single BLAHA storage site must not exceed 8,818 lb [4,000 kg]. An BLAHA may have multiple cells, but none can exceed 8,818 lb and each must be separated from adjacent sites by the applicable separation distance.

SCG and HCD criteria are somewhat relaxed for some AHA storage. AHA mixing rules for HCD require only that the NEW for all ammo in HCDs 1.1, 1.2 and 1.3 shall be added together and considered as HCD 1.1. The NEW for ammo classified as HCD 1.4 may be disregarded. Ammo classified as HCD/SCG 4.1G and 6.1G may also be stored in an AHA without restriction. Although the SCG and HCD criteria have been relaxed for AHA sites, storage should be in full compliance with peacetime storage criteria whenever possible.

ASP Storage

ASP storage sites are logistical storage locations for ammo that has not been issued to using units.

Typical ASP storage sites in a contingency environment include widely spaced open storage pads and protective construction using earthen berms or barricade systems such as HESCO Concertainer barricades and

steel bin barricades. Use of barricades will allow the sites (called cells or modules) to be located much closer together. Whether storage is open or barricaded, the storage sites should include environmental protection for the ammo such as MILVANs or ISO containers or, as a minimum, some sort of sun shading.

The maximum NEW that can be stored in ASP storage sites is 500,000 lb; however, real estate limitations generally will limit the maximum NEW to less. Compliance with SCG and HCD mixing rules is mandatory.

BLAHA Storage Table of Distances

NEQ/NEW on MILVAN Pad [1]	Distances (in meters)				
	A [2][4]	B	C [3]	D [4]	E [5]
500 kg (1,102 lb)	6.27	37.78	N/A	6.27	270.00
1,000 kg (2,205 lb)	7.90	47.60	N/A	7.90	270.00
1,500 kg (3,307 lb)	9.04	54.49	N/A	9.04	270.00
2,000 kg (4,409 lb)	9.95	59.97	N/A	9.95	270.00
2,500 kg (5,512 lb)	10.72	64.60	N/A	10.72	271.50
3,000 kg (6,614 lb)	11.39	68.65	N/A	11.39	297.41
3,500 kg (7,716 lb)	11.99	72.27	N/A	11.99	321.24
4,000 kg (8,818 lb)	12.54	75.56	N/A	12.54	343.42

NOTES:

(1) No separation between uploaded MILVANs on a pad is required. However, the MILVANs are expected to mass detonate. The net explosives quantity/net explosives weight (NEQ/NEW) is the total explosives weight of all the MILVANs on a single pad. NEQ/NEW is computed by combining all Ammo except small arms Ammo. AHA storage cannot exceed 4,000 kg per MILVAN pad.

(2) At this distance explosives are not expected to propagate but the munitions in adjacent pads will be unserviceable.

(3) A detonation at the MILVAN pad is not expected to propagate to the heavy armor. The closer the heavy armor is to the MILVAN pad the more likely the heavy armor will be damaged beyond serviceability.

(4) At these distances light armor may be damaged beyond serviceability.

(5) The presence of barricades does not reduce required external distances.

NOTE: BLAHA and Ready Ammo Storage Area (RASA) are exempt from ammunition compatibility requirements.

BLAHA Storage Distances

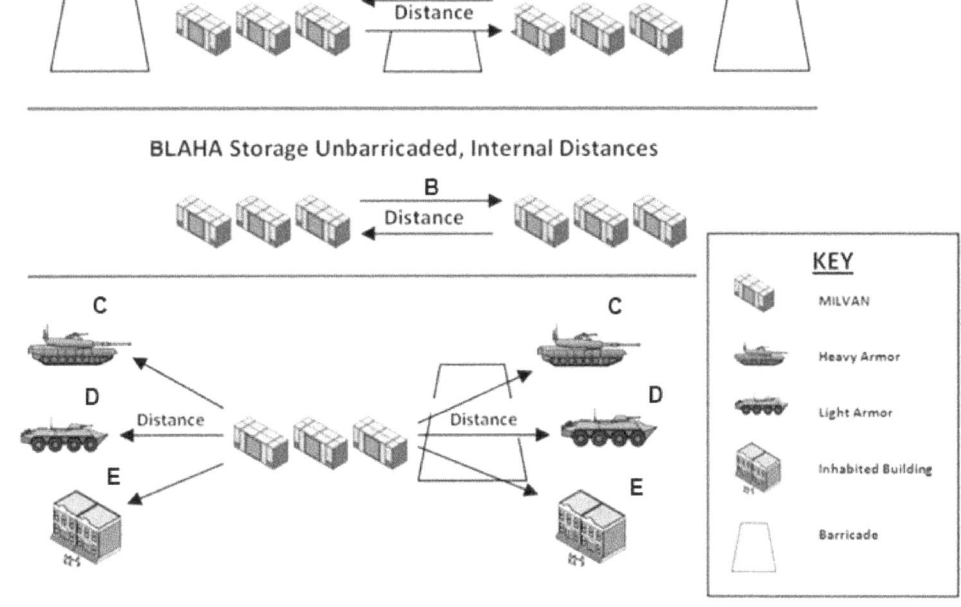

BLAHA Storage Using Barricades, Internal Distances

BLAHA Storage Unbarricaded, Internal Distances

KEY

MILVAN
Heavy Armor
Light Armor
Inhabited Building
Barricade

WARNING: THE PRESENCE OF BARRICADES DOES NOT REDUCE EXTERNAL DISTANCES.

AHA Configuration

Refer to these notes when viewing the AHA Configuration diagram on the following page:

Dimensions in red are critical dimensions.

(1) Nominal width of 6 MILVANS (each MILVAN 8' wide)

(2) Nominal length of MILVAN

(3) Improved approach apron recommended for forklift maneuvering (reduced maintenance cost)

(4) Minimum recommended roadway width to accommodate forklift maneuvering to/from MILVANS (greater distance recommended, see note 5)

(5) Minimum distance required MILVAN to MILVAN in adjacent cells is 28'. Practical considerations may require a greater distance (i.e. for roadways at front).

*Number of MILVANS may vary based on requirement; however, critical dimensions are the same.

**HESCO barricades depicted in this drawing are the recommended configuration. Other configurations are permissible provided the configuration is stable and provides a minimum height of 10'. Although minimum barricade height is 1' above line-of-sight from top of MILVANS in adjacent cells, a 10' to 10.5' barricade height will account for a slight elevation of the MILVAN pads for

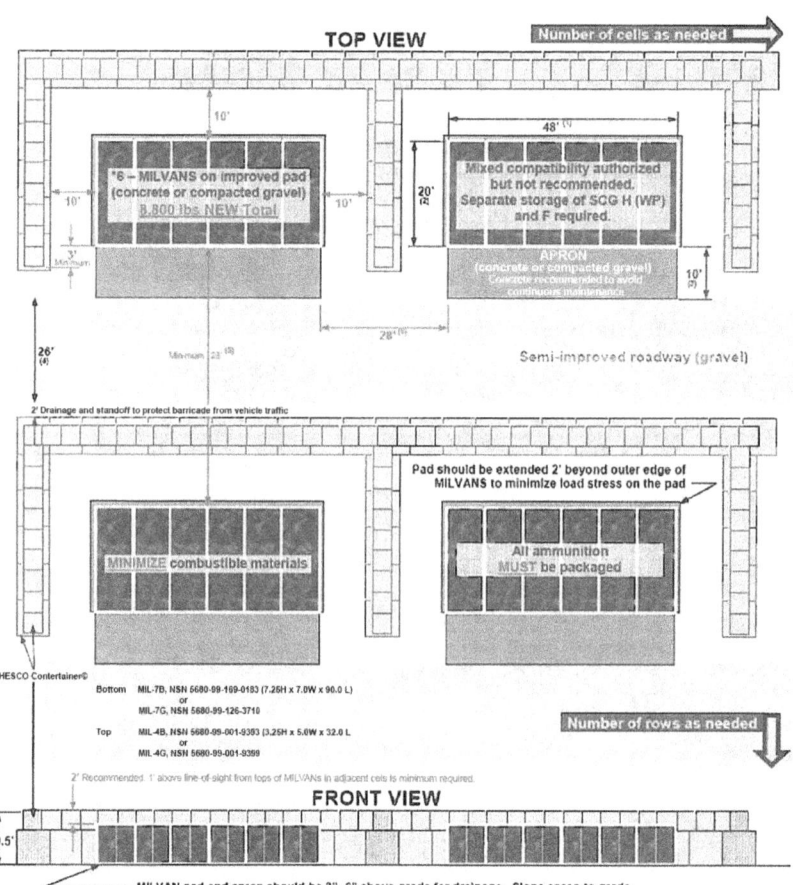

Earth-Filled Steel Bin Barricades

Earth-filled steel bin barricades are designed and approved to reduce the IMD between ammo storage cells. There are two types of steel bin barricades:

OPTION 1 Revetments
- Must be a minimum of 7 ft [2.1 m] thick
- Can be used to limit an MCE in a series of cells to the largest quantity in a single cell, provided the quantity in the single cell does not exceed 30,000 lb NEW

OPTION 2 Revetments
- Must be a minimum of 5.25 ft [1.6 m] thick
- Can be similarly used to limit the MCE, provided no cell contains more than 5,000 lb NEW

When properly sited, these cells prevent prompt propagation; however, all assets in the series of cells are at risk of loss. Although a revetment is effective in limiting the blast, there is a significant probability that the

contents of many of the cells will be damaged or destroyed by the initial and subsequent fire and explosions. The extent of such losses increases with the amount of explosives present.

For steel bin barricades to be used effectively, the following conditions must be met:

- Ammo shall be positioned no closer than 10 ft [3.1 m] from cell walls, no closer than 3 ft [0.9 m] from the end of the wing walls, and no higher than 2 ft [0.6 m] below the top of cell walls.
- Ammo shall be distributed over the available area within the cell, rather than being concentrated in a small area.
- Ammo stored in a cell in quantities near the maximum NEW limit shall not be positioned in a single row of pallets, stacks or trailers.
- The storage of ammo in flammable outer-pack configurations, such as wood boxes, shall be minimized.
- The types of ammo to be stored in these type areas shall be verified with Quality Assurance Specialist Ammunition Surveillance (QASAS) or Explosives Safety personnel to ensure compliance with standards.
- 1,250 feet external arc for IBD/PTRD

Steel Bin Barricade

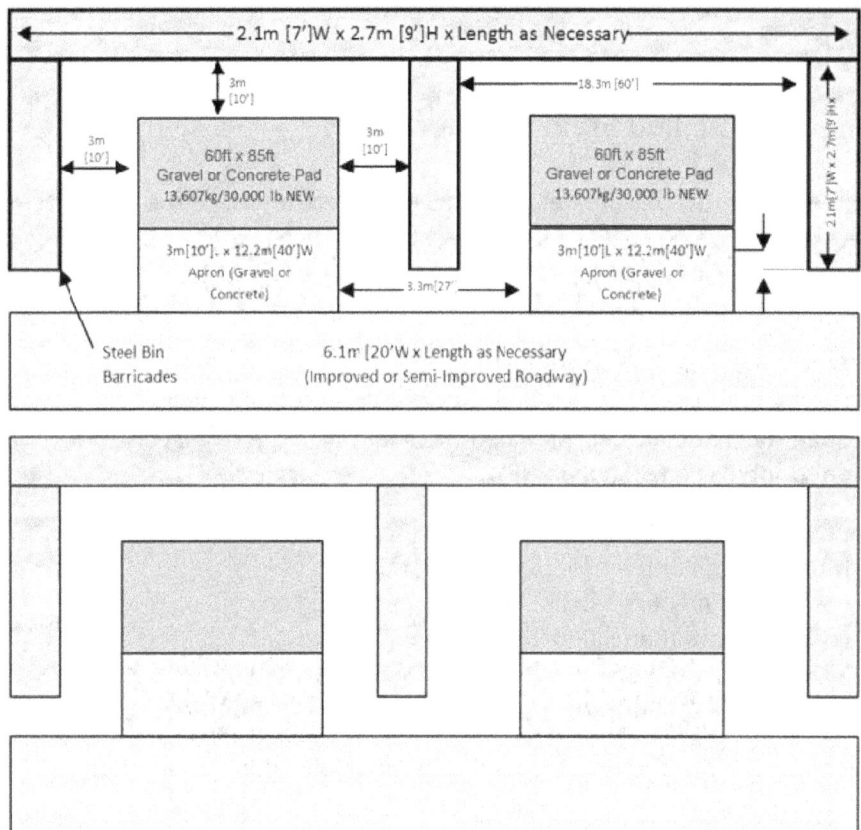

Arms Rooms

Compliance with QD and compatibility criteria is not required for mission essential or operationally necessary quantities of ammo in HCD 1.4 or 6.1 (excluding toxic chemical munitions). In addition, up to 100 lb NEW HCD 1.3 and up to 50 lb NEW HD 1.2.2 may be stored in this manner. However, a composite risk management worksheet shall be prepared according to FM 5-19 and will be submitted with an explosives storage license for consideration by the approving official. Documentation of the risk assessment will be maintained in the designated safety office. Documentation of the risk assessment will be part of the license and maintained with all copies of the license.

Light Armor Vehicles

Vehicles designed to resist small arms ammunition fire and fragmentation from artillery shell detonations are considered light armor. They include:

- High Mobility Multi-purpose Wheeled Vehicle (HMMWV) with Frag-5 or comparable kits
- M1117 Armor Security Vehicle (ASV)
- Mine Resistant Ambush Protected (MRAP) vehicle, including Buffalo and RG-31
- M109/FAASV
- M113 series vehicles
- Striker vehicle family

These vehicles are not designed to contain explosions within the vehicles, but are designed to protect contents and passengers from outside blasts/ fragmentation. This design will prevent propagation via high speed, low angle fragmentation between vehicles, but will not prevent the vehicle from coming apart in the event of an explosion. For this reason, a light armored vehicle is treated as barricaded as an ES and un-barricaded as a PES.

Separation distances are based on ammo being stored in the interior armored compartment with the door and other openings closed while parked in an authorized location. If ammo is stored in compartments external to the crew compartment, the ammo is not afforded "Light Armor" protection and is considered "Non-Armor." An example is a light armored vehicle that is approximately 7m long by 3m wide, if there are 5 of these vehicles parked together, side by side, with 110.2 lb NEW of HCD 1.1 ammo stored 'under armor' in each, your internal footprint would be approximately 2.91m between vehicles, making your parking area footprint 7m by 26.64m (5 vehicles times 3m and 4 spaces between them of 2.91m each). The external distance would be 277m by 296.64m (add 270m to each figure).

See the next table for internal separation.

Separation distance is measured from the outside edge of the vehicle, not from the edge of the uploaded munitions.

Light Armor Vehicles Table of Distances
(Distances in meters)

NEQ/NEW [1] [4] per Light Armor Vehicle	Spacing [2] between Vehicles	Spacing [2] from Non Armor Vehicles	External [3] Distance
2 kg (4.4 lb)	0.99	4.75	270
3 kg (6.6 lb)	1.14	4.97	270
4 kg (8.8 lb)	1.25	5.13	270
5 kg (11 lb)	1.35	5.26	270
10 kg (22 lb)	1.70	5.68	270
20 kg (44 lb)	2.14	6.14	270
30 kg (66.1 lb)	2.45	6.42	270
40 kg (88.2 lb)	2.70	6.63	270
50 kg (110.2 lb)	2.91	6.80	270

NOTES:
(1) The NEQ/NEW is the total explosives weight of all ammo on a vehicle. NEQ/NEW includes all ammo combined, treated as HCD 1.1 (exclude HCD 1.4 materials (small arms)).
(2) At this distance explosives are not expected to propagate. At these distances light armor or non-armor may be damaged beyond serviceability.
(3) The presence of barricades does not reduce required external distances.
(4) Design of vehicle should provide equal barricading.

Forward Arming and Refueling Point (FARP)

The template on the next page depicts a FARP at an OCONUS installation. The concept of the operation is that the Rearm Pads resupply the helicopters, the Ready Ammunition Storage Area (RASA) resupplies the Rearm Pads and the aviation Ammunition Holding Area (AHA) supplies the RASAs. The Rearm Pads should be located between helicopter landing sites for ease of loading. Internal distance is required from the FARP to the RASA and to the AHA. Additional RASA sites could be added but each RASA must be separated from other RASAs by a minimum of internal distance.

Armament pads will contain the minimum amount to conduct efficient operations. In no case will the amount of munitions exceed what is required to arm the maximum number of helicopters that can be refueled at one time.

NOTE: Commanders should carefully weigh the risks of "Efficient Operations" when those operations adversely affect internal and external QD standards.

WARNING: Locate fuel downhill from ammunition!

FARP Diagram

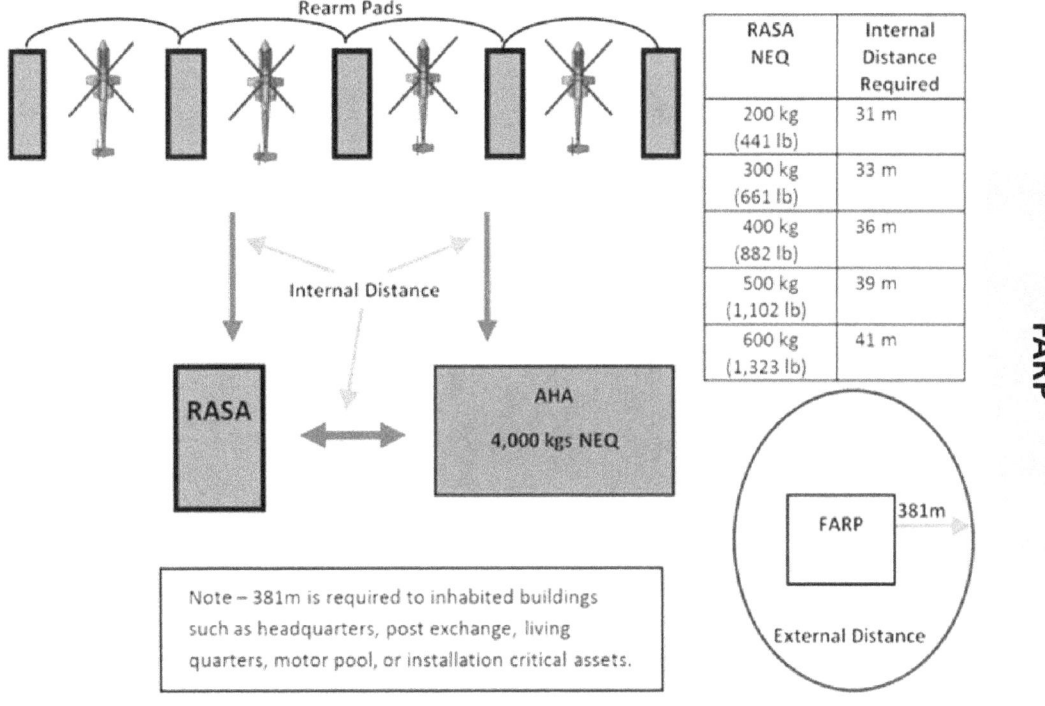

RASA NEQ	Internal Distance Required
200 kg (441 lb)	31 m
300 kg (661 lb)	33 m
400 kg (882 lb)	36 m
500 kg (1,102 lb)	39 m
600 kg (1,323 lb)	41 m

Rearm Pads

Internal Distance

RASA

AHA
4,000 kgs NEQ

Note – 381m is required to inhabited buildings such as headquarters, post exchange, living quarters, motor pool, or installation critical assets.

FARP   381m

External Distance

Combat Aircraft Parking Area (CAPA)

Special consideration must be given to plans where contingency operations employ the use of ammo. Commanders must apply Composite Risk Management when approving these plans. The proper use of such features as barricades or earth-filled, steel-bin-type barricades (ARMCO, Inc. revetment or equivalent) can decrease the magnitude of a potential event and increase the explosives capacity of limited areas.

For aircraft other than Army aircraft and for asset preservation, PTRD is required (i.e. HCD 1.1 material, use 60% of IBD, for HCD 1.2, 1.3 or 1.4 apply standard PTRD distance). PTRD may not provide protection from fragments. To protect against low-angle, high-energy fragments, aircraft should be properly barricaded (see Barricades section).

For loaded aircraft to loaded aircraft, measure the shortest distance between explosives on one aircraft to explosives on the adjacent aircraft.

Barricades could be used to increase the allowable explosives limits. However, concrete traffic barricades (T-walls, Texas and Jersey barriers) have not been evaluated for explosives safety purposes and would not be considered barricades. HESCO Concertainers or Steel Bin Barricades (soil/

sand/dirt filled) are considered adequate barricades but could be a source of foreign object debris (FOD) on airfields.

Certificate of Risk Acceptance (CoRA)

Every effort should be made to comply with explosives safety requirements. If the minimum explosives safety quantity distances, either internal or external, cannot be obtained, then the situation calls for a Certificate of Risk Acceptance (CoRA). The CoRA took the place of a waiver or exemption. A CoRA can also be used for other explosives safety deficiencies such as lack of lightning protection for ammunition storage or risk to mission capability (i.e. less than PTRD). Information on explosives safety CoRAs is contained in DA PAM 385-30.

Commonly Asked Questions Regarding CoRAs:

1. Who should prepare an explosives safety CoRA?

Anyone can prepare a CoRA for a Commander. The Originating Unit is responsible for initiating the CoRA. Generally, the Safety Officer or QASAS prepares or assists in the preparation of the CoRA form, but ultimately, the responsibility falls to whomever the Commander appoints to the task.

2. What information is required?

    a. A good scale map that shows:
- Location of the ammo or uploaded vehicles

- Entire area of the external footprint
- Information on all structures within the external footprint
- Information on any local national structures within the external footprint

b. Information on the number of people that are routinely within that external footprint and the value of structures within that external footprint. If this information is not easily available, make best estimates.

3. Who can approve an explosives safety CoRA?

The level of approval for an explosives safety CoRA depends on two factors, the level of risk and the duration of that risk. Low and medium risk explosives safety CoRAs can be approved by the installation or Garrison Commander. However, risks lasting for greater than a year will typically be accepted at the General Officer level. Usually, the level of command that has the resources to implement "the fix" will be the approving authority. If that General Officer does not control the assets necessary to fix the deficiency, then the CoRA would need to be approved at the higher level that does control the assets (see Table 4-2, DA PAM 385-30 for specific approval authority).

4. If an explosives safety CoRA includes hazards to other service personnel or local nationals, do you need to coordinate with those at risk?

Yes. In the case of other US services (Navy, Air Force or Marine Corps), inform their command if Army explosives storage or operations puts their personnel or assets at risk. If the other Service's explosives storage puts Army troop assets at risk, they need to coordinate their risk acceptance document with you. In the case of local nationals, seek the advice of legal counsel.

NOTE: Risk has to be accepted by commanders at equivalent grades or positions from all services affected.

Explosives Licenses

All ammo locations must be "licensed" for the type of location and type and amount of explosives allowed there. This is a "locally" generated document in that it is developed and approved by the appropriate knowledgeable personnel immediately up the chain of command.

The purpose of an explosives license is to ensure that a person with explosives safety knowledge and training is satisfied that the location, type and amount of ammo allowed meet the approved explosives safety requirements.

Though there is no specific form to be used for this, the minimum types of information required are:

- Ammunition or explosives area (operating base, etc.) location.
- Ammunition or explosives facility location (where is it on the operating base).
- The type of facility (shipping container, arms room, storage pad, etc.).
- The types of HD authorized to be there (HD 1.1, HD 1.2.1, HD 1.2.2, HD 1.3, HD 1.4).

- The allowable limits of each HD (in lb or kg).
- Determining factor or object which limits the amount of ammo allowed (what is the exposed site causing that particular limitation).
- The actual separation distance (ft or m) between the location being licensed and the ES causing that limitation.

Explosives Safety Assistance

Explosives safety assistance can be obtained from Command Safety personnel or QASAS personnel, usually located at the ammunition supply point or with the supporting logistics cell.

If additional assistance is needed, contact the Command Safety Office and request assistance from the US Army Technical Center for Explosives Safety (USATCES) at:

> usarmy.mcalester.usamc.list.dac-es
> DSN: 956-8919; 956-8737; 956-8745
> Commercial: 918-420-8737

Additional explosives safety information can be found on the "Explosives Safety Ammunition Toolbox" link on the US Army Technical Center for Explosives Safety website: https://www3.dac.army.mil.

Acronyms

A&E—Ammunition and Explosives (collectively referred to as "ammo" in this booklet)

AAFES—Army and Air Force Exchange Service

AGM—Above Ground Magazine

AHA—Ammunition Holding Area

AR—Army Regulation

ASP—Ammunition Supply Point

ASV—Armor Security Vehicle

ATHP—Ammunition Transfer and Holding Area

BLAHA—Basic Load Ammunition Holding Area

CEA—Captured Enemy Ammunition

CoRA—Certificate of Risk Acceptance

CSA—Corps Storage Areas

DA PAM—Department of the Army Pamphlet

DAC—Defense Ammunition Center

DDESB—Department of Defense Explosives Safety Board

DLSC—Defense Logistics Services Center

DOD—Department of Defense

DODIC—Department of Defense Identification Code

ECM—Earth Covered Magazines

EOD—Explosive Ordnance Disposal

ES—Exposed Site

ESQD—Explosives Safety Quantity Distance

FARP—Forward Arming and Refueling Point

FOD—Foreign Object Debris

HC—Hazard Classes

HCD—Hazard Class/Division

HCL—Hazard Classification Listing

HMMWV—High Mobility Multi-Purpose Wheeled Vehicle

IBD—Inhabited Building Distance

ILD—IntraLine Distance

IMD—Intermagazine Distance

ISO—International Standards Organization

JERRV—Joint Explosive Ordnance Disposal Rapid Response Vehicle (Cougar)

JHCS—Joint Hazard Classification System

MACOM—Major Army Command

MCE—Maximum Creditable Event

MOOTW—Military Operations Other Than War

MRAP—Mine Resistant Ambush Protected (Buffalo, RG-31)

MWR—Morale, Welfare and Recreation

NEQ—Net Explosives Quantity (in kg)

NEW—Net Explosive Weight (in lb)

PES—Potential Explosion Site

PTR—Public Traffic Route

QASAS—Quality Assurance Specialist (Ammunition Surveillance)

QD—Quantity Distance

RASA—Ready Ammunition Storage Area

SCG—Storage Compatibility Groups

TSA—Theater Storage Areas

UNO—United Nations Organization

Glossary

AHA Storage Sites—Locations where ammo that has been issued to using units can be safely stored.

ASP Storage Sites—Logistical storage locations for ammo that has not been issued to using units.

Certificate of Risk Acceptance (CoRA)—Document needed if the minimum explosives safety quantity distances, either internal or external, cannot be obtained.

Combat Aircraft Parking Area (CAPA)—A parking area for aircraft uploaded with ammo to be available for quick reaction.

Delayed Propagation—This occurs when an ammo site unintentionally blows up and causes adjacent ammo to blow up or burn for a few seconds to hours later.

Department of Defense Identification Code (DODIC)—A four-digit code assigned by the Defense Logistics Services Center (DLSC); used to find the NEW.

Exposed Site—This is any location that might be affected by an unintentional detonation at an adjacent PES.

External Distance—Required for the separation of personnel and facilities that are outside the confines of an ammo storage area and that are not

directly related or associated with the ammo storage area mission.

Forward Arming and Refueling Point (FARP)—A temporary arming and refueling facility that an aviation unit commander organizes, equips and deploys to support combat tactical operations.

Hazard Class/Division—A numerical designator within an HC indicating the character and predominance of associated hazards and the potential for causing personnel casualties and property damage.

Hazardous Fragment—A fragment having an impact energy of 58 ft-lbs or greater. This 58 ft-lb impact energy was determined to be the energy required to take a soldier out of action (very likely a fatality).

Inhabited Building—Any location where personnel not associated with the ammo area may gather. It can include troop billets, mess halls, MWR facilities, maintenance shops, etc.

Inhabited Building Distance—Distance maintained between a PES and an inhabited building; provides excellent protection to personnel and material assets from blast effects and very good protection from fragments.

Intermagazine Distance—Distance required between two ammo storage locations, used to prevent explosive propagation from one location to another.

Internal Distances—Required for the separation of operating facilities and storage sites within the confines of an Ammo storage area.

Intraline Distance—Distance maintained from a PES to an associated ES; can be barricaded or unbarricaded. Applied to Ammo operations such as Ammo surveillance and Ammo maintenance.

Joint Hazard Classification System (JHCS)—The official source for determining the HCD and NEW for Ammo items.

Light Armor Vehicles—Vehicles that are designed to resist small arms ammunition fire and fragmentation from artillery shell detonations.

Measuring Distances—Distances should be measured from the exterior edge of any Ammo storage site or Ammo operating facility to the nearest edge of any exposure being considered.

Minimum Hazardous Fragment Distance—The distance at which the areal density of hazardous fragments or debris becomes one per 600 ft^2. At this distance, there is a 1% probability of a person being hit by a hazardous fragment (1% Lethality Distance).

Net Explosive Weight (NEW)—The actual weight in pounds of explosive mixtures or compounds; used in determining explosive limits and explosive quantity data arcs.

Operating Facilities—Can include workshops, reconfiguration operations, minor maintenance operations, issue/turn-in operations, administrative office spaces directly related to the Ammo mission, etc.

Prompt Propagation—This occurs when one ammo site unintentionally blows up and at the same time causes another ammo site to blow up.

Public Traffic Route—Any road or street on a military post used by the general public, a passenger carrying railroad, or a waterway capable of being used by ships or barges; also used to describe the amount of protection required by other ES from an unintentional explosion.

Public Traffic Route Distance—Provides less protection with a higher probability of serious injuries and fatalities.

Quantity Distance—The application of the rules on separation to ensure the proper degree of protection for personnel and assets.

Rogue Fragment—A hazardous fragment projected beyond the minimum hazardous fragment distance (to a distance at which the areal density of hazardous fragments or debris is less than one per 600 ft^2); i.e., a fragment thrown from an explosion much further than would normally be expected.

Steel Bin Barricade—Earth-filled steel bins used to separate ammo.

Storage Compatibility Group—A letter designation assigned to indicate what may be stored or transported together.

Storage Site—Can include MILVANS, ISO Containers, Open Pads, ARMAG Containers, etc.

Yellow Book—An unofficial source for determining HCD and NEW.

Glossary